ADVENTURES OF THE LUNGS

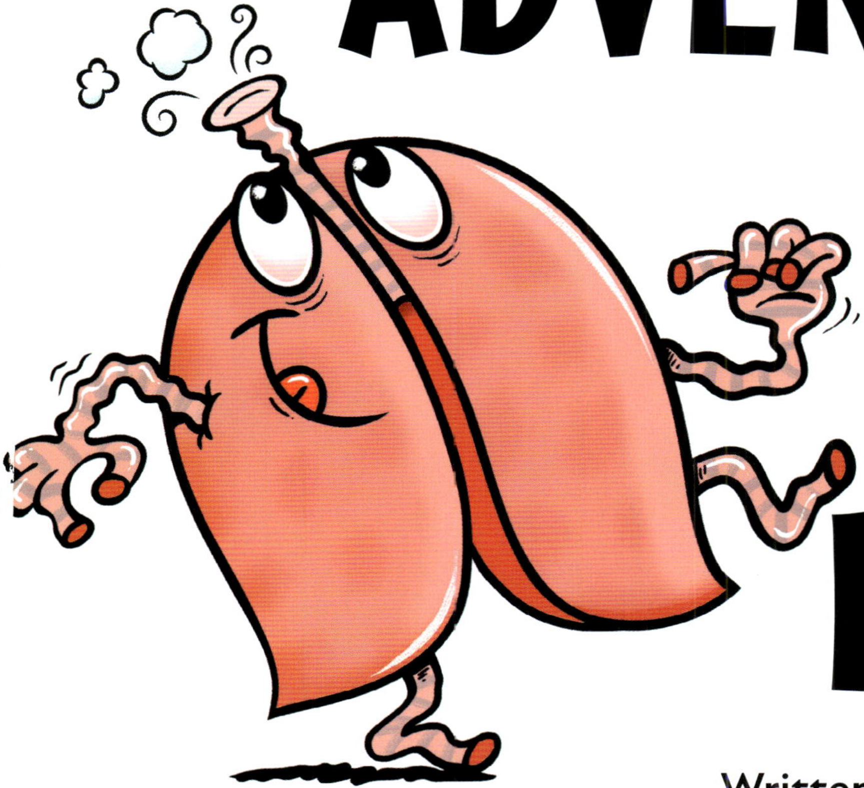

Written by Dr Numbere K Numbere
Illustrated by Gary Boller

WAYLAND

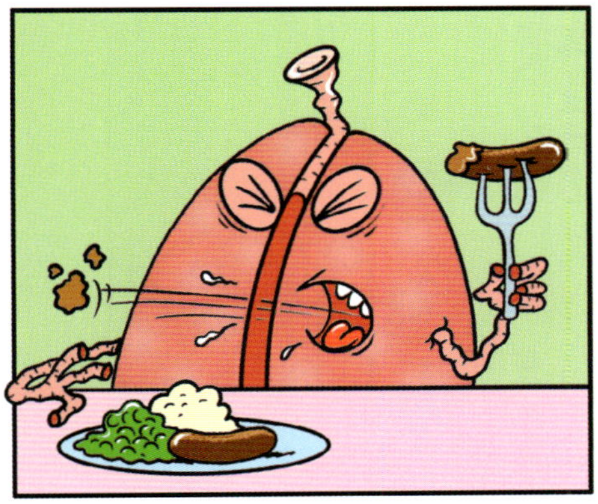

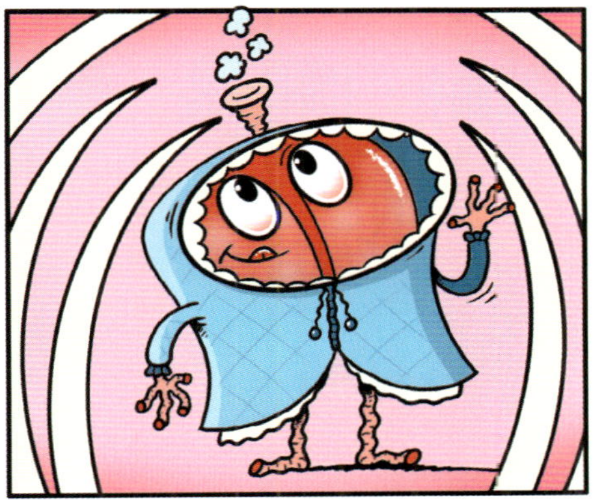

First published in Great Britain in 2026 by Wayland

Project editor: Claire Sipi
Illustration and Design: Gary Boller

ISBN: 978 1 5263 2859 5 HBK
ISBN: 978 1 5263 2860 1 PBK

Printed and bound in Dubai

Wayland, an imprint of
Hachette Children's Group
Part of Hodder and Stoughton Limited
Carmelite House
50 Victoria Embankment
London EC4Y 0DZ

An Hachette UK Company
www.hachette.co.uk
www.hachettechildrens.co.uk

The authorised representative in the EEA is Hachette Ireland,
8 Castlecourt Centre, Dublin 15, D15 XTP3, Ireland
(email: info@hbgi.ie)

MIX
Paper | Supporting responsible forestry
FSC® C104740

CONTENTS

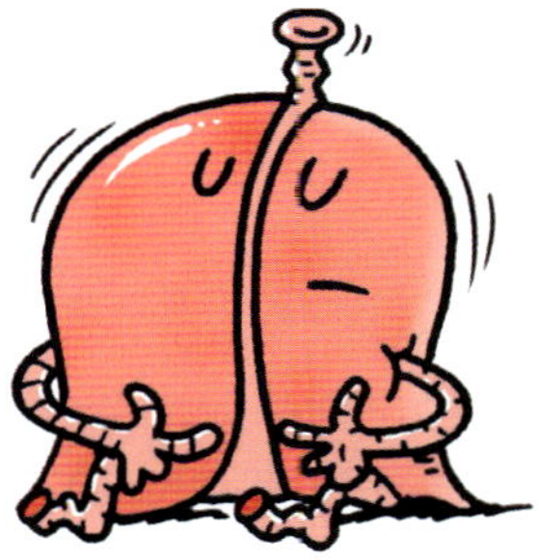

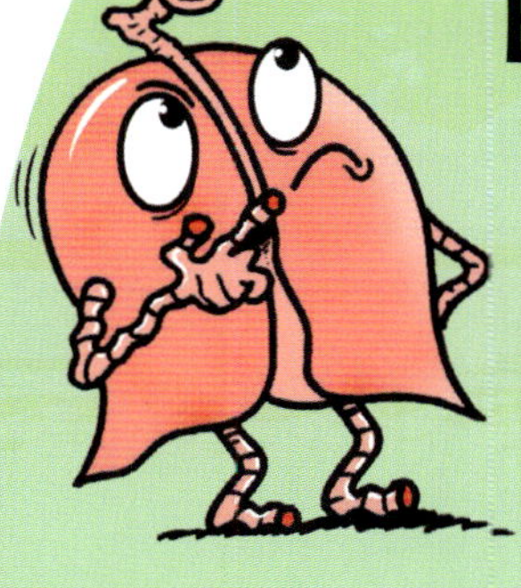

WHAT ARE THE LUNGS?

DID YOU KNOW?

The word 'lung' literally means 'the light organ'? Lungs are full of air and would float in water!

The lungs are a part of a team called the respiratory system with organs that all work towards helping us breathe. Without these spongy organs, we would not be able to use the air we breathe.

The lungs are like a gas pumping station, transporting oxygen into your bloodstream and moving carbon dioxide out.

The lungs help us absorb oxygen from the air we breathe. Oxygen (O_2) is the fuel for the body – we need oxygen to create the energy we need to be able to do, well anything at all.

At the same time, the lungs help us to also remove a waste gas called carbon dioxide (CO_2) from the body. The lungs are very hardworking!

THE RESPIRATORY SYSTEM

All these parts make up the respiratory system.

We have two lungs in our chest. The right lung has three lobes: the upper lobe, the middle lobe and the lower lobe, while the left lung has the upper lobe and the lower lobe. The left lung is smaller than the right lung to make room for the heart.

The lungs themselves are very well protected by the ribcage – it truly is a protective cage formed of 12 ribs connected to the spine (verterbrae) and the breastbone (sternum).

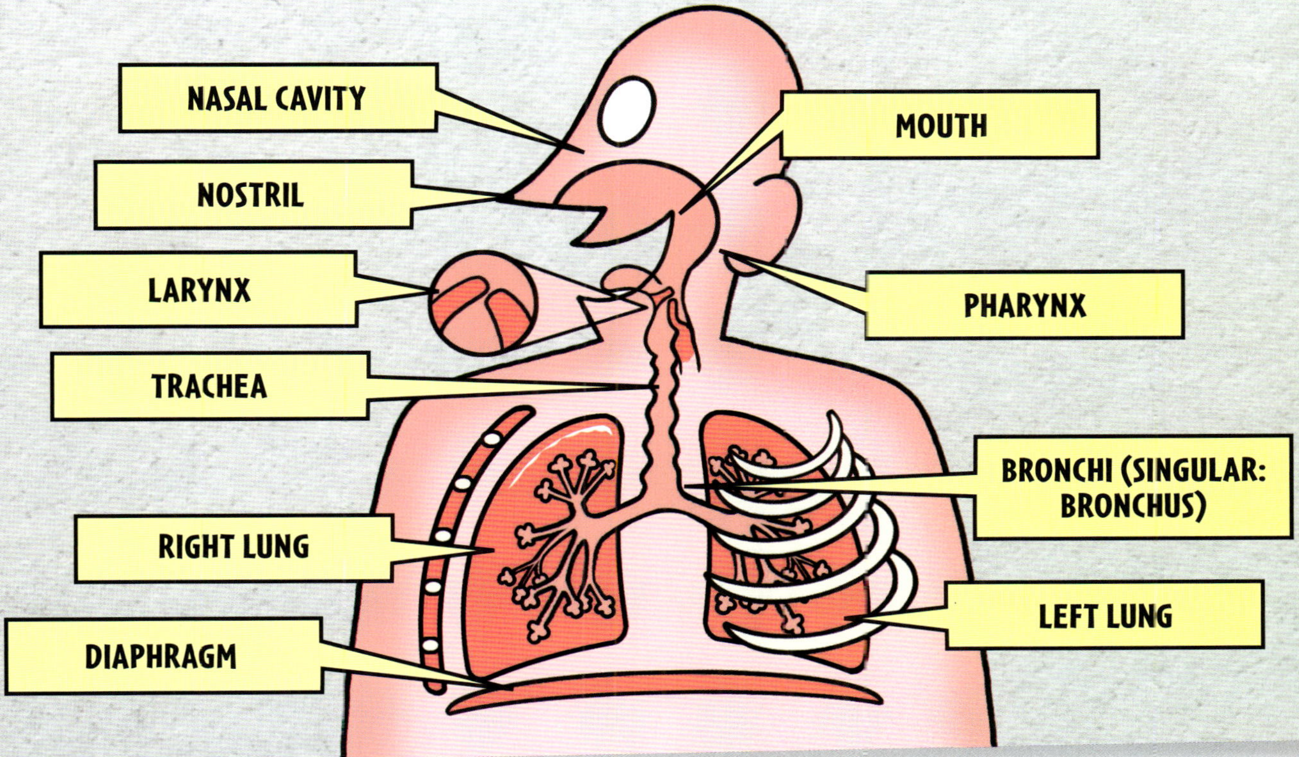

As well as having the ribcage to protect them, the lungs are each covered by a pair of thin membranes called the pleura.

The pleura cushions them against the ribs when they inflate with air and provide an extra layer of protection from outside damage.

HOW DO WE BREATHE?

So how does air get to the lungs anyway? Let's find out. Our adventure begins at the nose.

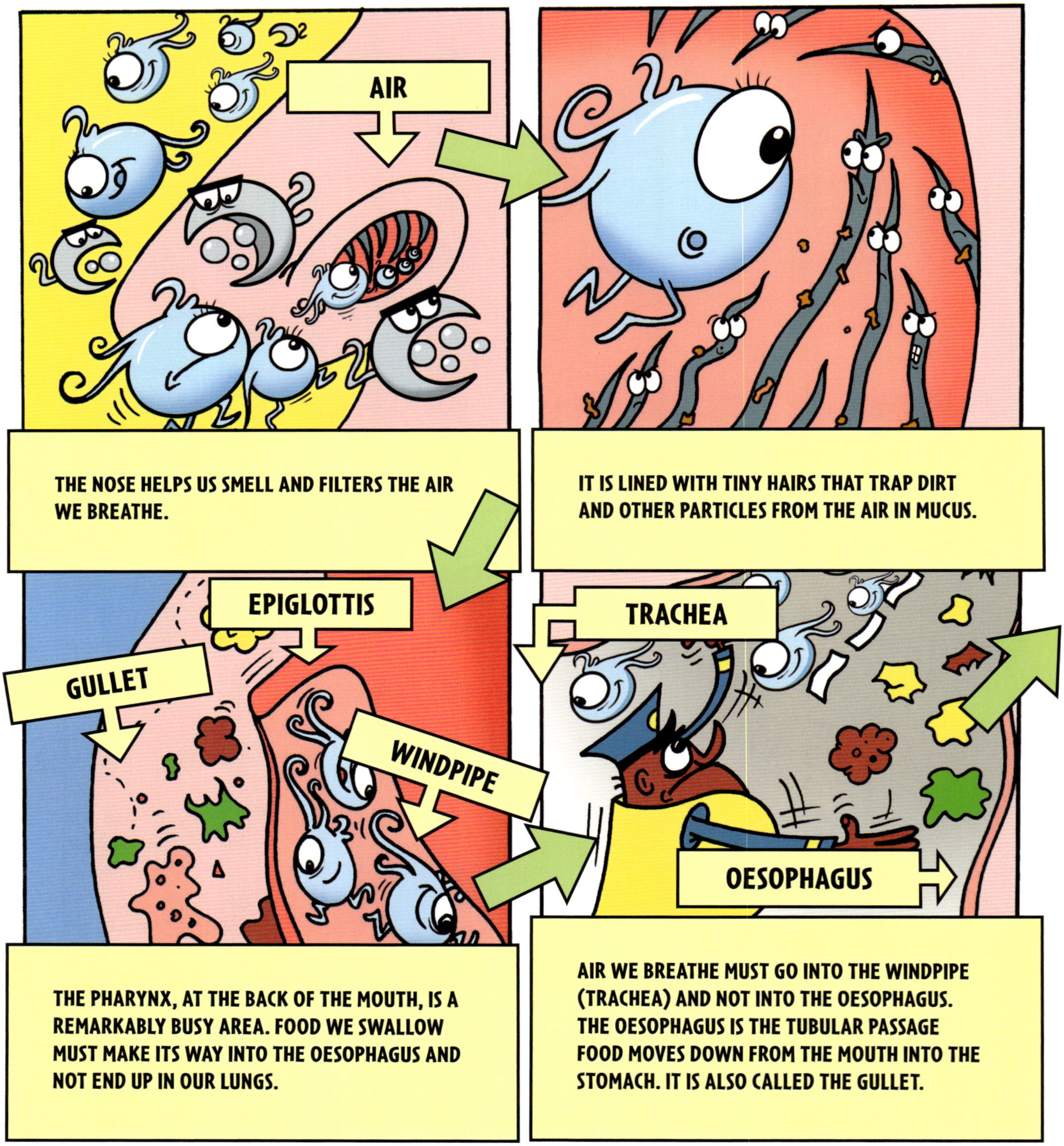

AT THE SAME TIME, UP TO 1.5 LITRES (OR SIX GLASSES) OF SALIVA IS PRODUCED AND SWALLOWED EVERY DAY. SOUNDS LIKE A LOT OF TRAFFIC ON A SLIPPERY ROAD!

The epiglottis is a flap of muscle that covers the windpipe when we swallow so food does not go the wrong way and cause choking. It is relaxed when we breathe so air can get past the vocal cords and into the windpipe.

This is why your parents tell you not to talk while you're eating – talking is essentially a version of breathing out and so food can end up in the windpipe if you eat and talk at the same time.

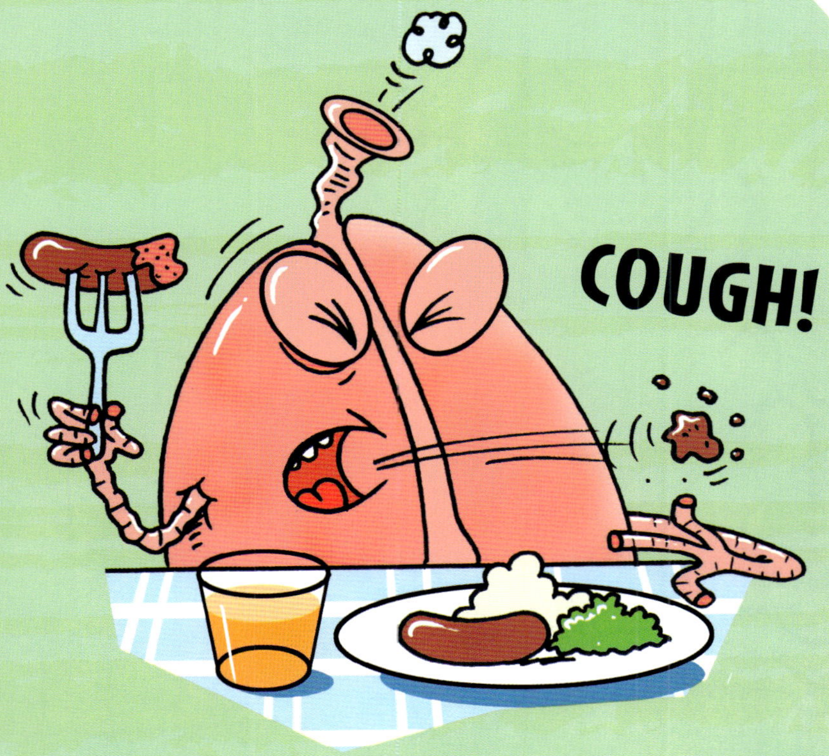

DID YOU KNOW?

Your nose and your eyes are connected! That is why it is sometimes possible to taste eyedrops. Tiny holes in the corner of your eyes (called puncta) drain excess tears through a duct into the back of the nose. And the back of the nose leads into the throat.

JOURNEY DOWN THE THROAT TO THE LUNGS

We are now in the larynx, which sits at the top of the windpipe. The larynx is also called the voice box, and this is where the vocal cords lie. These are bands of muscle that act as the gates of the windpipe keeping any unwanted material out.

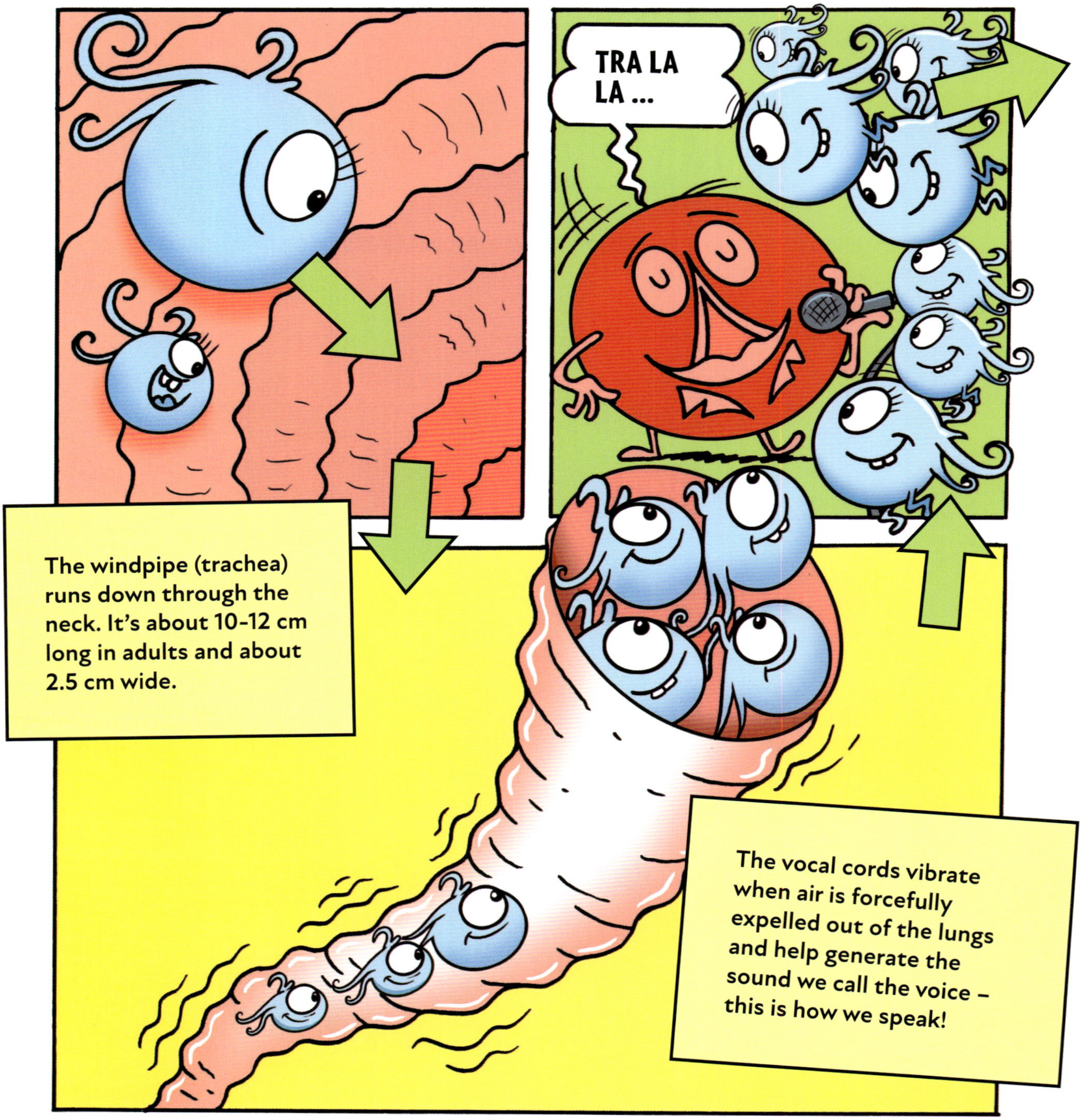

Many of the cells that line the inside of the windpipe have tiny hair-like structures called cilia. These cilia move in a wave-like motion, sweeping mucus up the windpipe and into the throat, where it is coughed up, sneezed out or swallowed.

The mucus is sticky and catches many of the germs, dust and other matter that has been breathed in, to stop it invading and harming the lungs.

The windpipe is protected on its outside by hard rings of cartilage that you can feel in the front of your neck. The rings do not run all the way around so that there is room for the oesophagus, which lies behind the windpipe. The oesophagus needs to be able to stretch when swallowing food.

At its base, at a ridge of cartilage called the carina of trachea, the windpipe eventually divides into two main air tubes: the right and left bronchi.

LEFT BRONCHUS

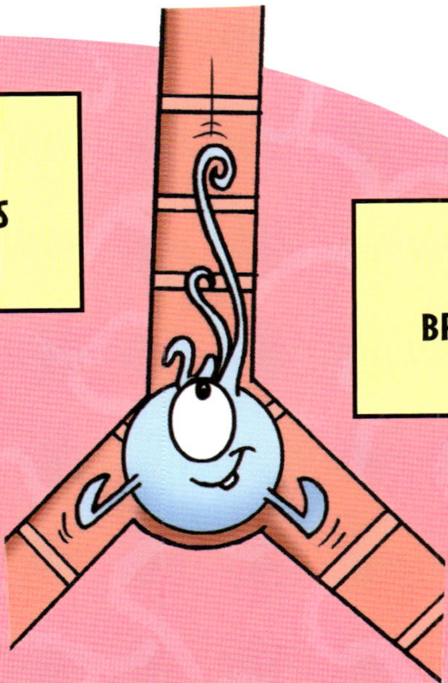

RIGHT BRONCHUS

DID YOU KNOW?

Human vocal cords can vibrate as fast as up to 1,000 times a second!

INSIDE THE LUNGS

Air enters the lungs along the windpipe and through the left bronchus and the right bronchus. Inside each lung, each bronchus divides again and again into more bronchi. Smaller, narrower air tubes called bronchioles which branch off the bronchi. These bronchioles end in groups of tiny air sacs called alveoli.

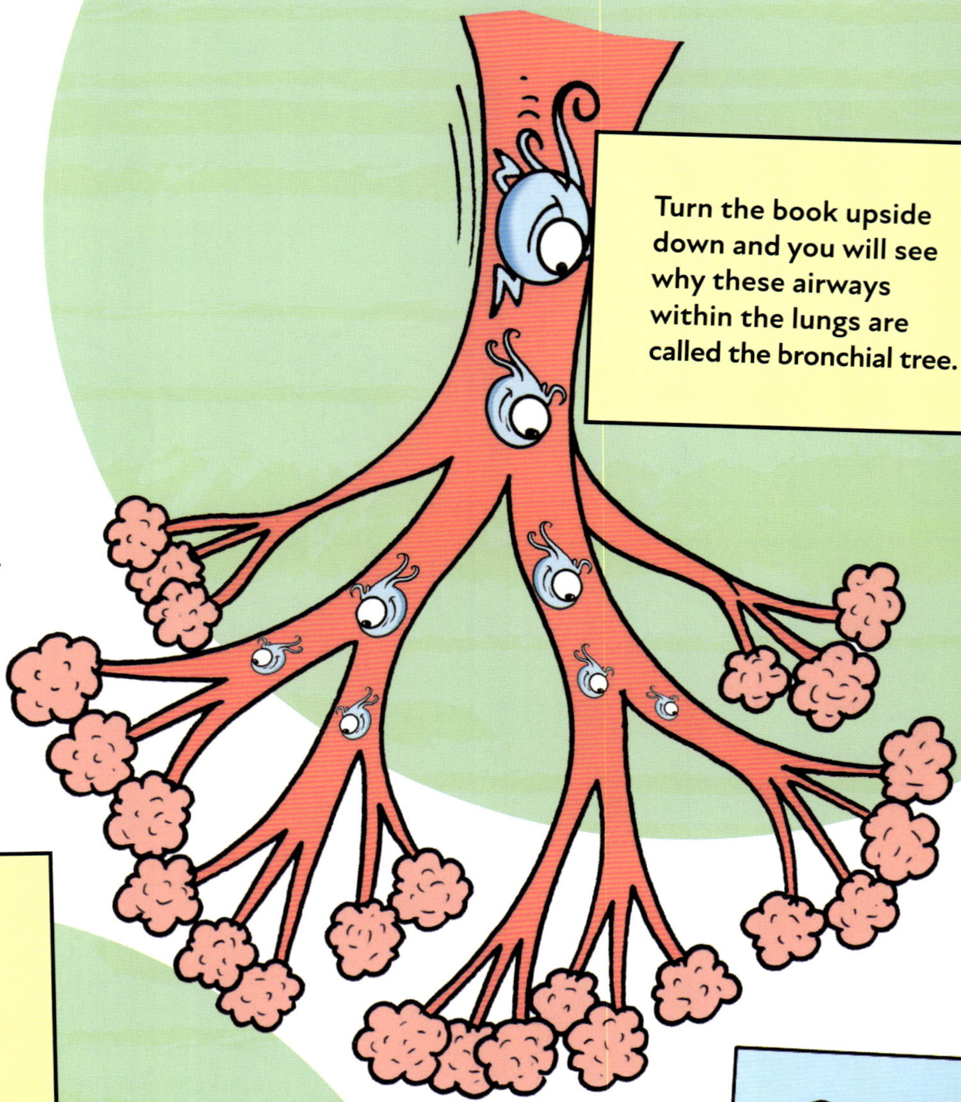

Turn the book upside down and you will see why these airways within the lungs are called the bronchial tree.

If the airways are the trunk and branches of the lungs, then the alveoli, also called the air sacs, are the leaves!

DID YOU KNOW?

The total length of the airways inside the lungs if they were all laid out end to end is about 2,414 km! That's more than the distance from London, England to Athens, Greece.

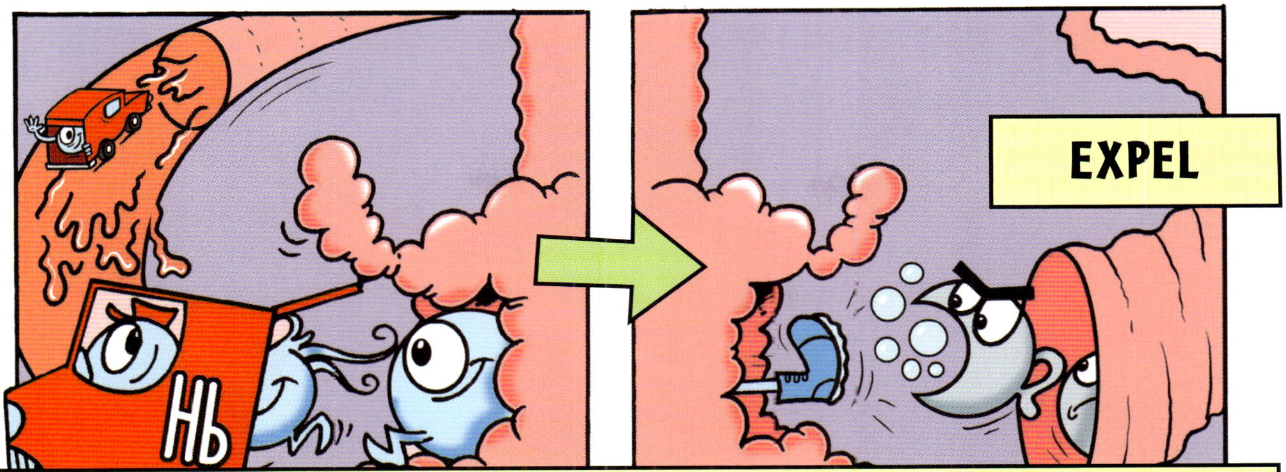

THE AIR SACS ARE WHERE OXYGEN IS TRANSFERRED INTO THE BLOODSTREAM FOR TRANSPORTATION TO THE HEART AND WHERE CARBON DIOXIDE IS TRANSFERRED FROM BLOOD TO THE AIR SACS FOR EXHALATION.

THERE ARE OVER 300 MILLION ALVEOLI IN EACH LUNG, EACH LINED INSIDE WITH A SOAP-LIKE SUBSTANCE CALLED SURFACTANT. THIS PREVENTS THE WALLS OF THE ALVEOLI FROM STICKING TOGETHER.

THE ALVEOLI ARE ARRANGED IN A PATTERN THAT IS VERY MUCH LIKE A STEM OF BROCCOLI OR A CLUSTER OF (SOAPY!) GRAPES!

IF ALL THE ALVEOLI IN THE LUNGS OF AN AVERAGE ADULT WERE SPREAD OUT FLAT ALONGSIDE EACH OTHER, THEY WOULD COVER OVER HALF OF A TENNIS COURT!

HOW THE LUNGS WORK

DID YOU KNOW?

Dolphins can hold their breath for up to an impressive 20 minutes at a time, thanks to their large lungs and efficient use of oxygen.

SUPER MUSCLE!

The diaphragm is the main muscle involved in breathing.

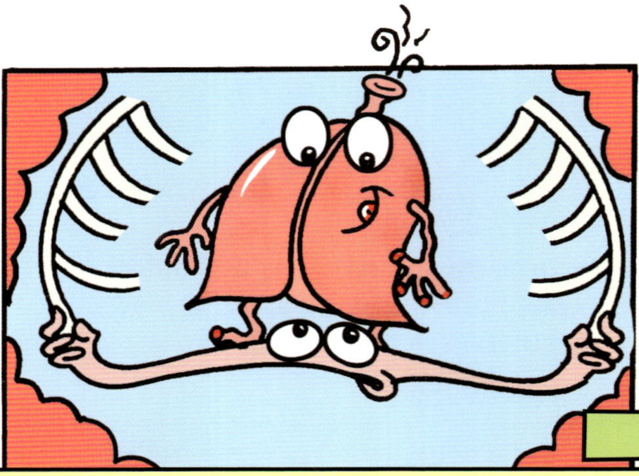

IT IS A THIN, DOME-SHAPED MUSCLE.
IT STRETCHES ACROSS THE BASE OF THE CHEST BELOW THE LUNGS AND HEART AND IS ATTACHED TO THE STERNUM, SEVERAL POINTS ON THE BOTTOM OF THE RIBCAGE AND TO THE SPINE.

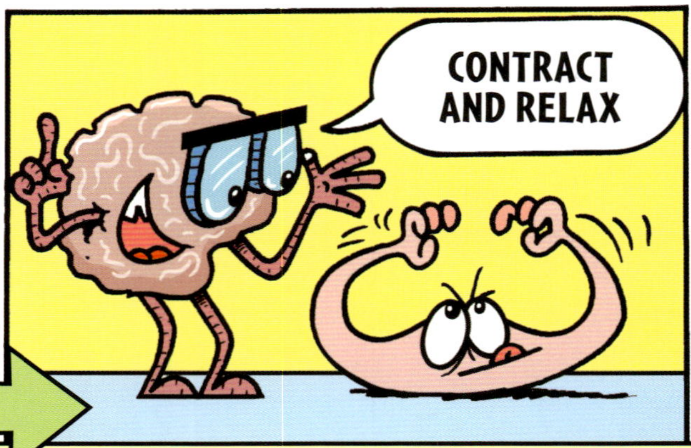

THE DIAPHRAGM RESPONDS TO MESSAGES FROM THE BRAIN.

IT IS A SUPER-MUSCLE – IT IS ONE OF THE HARDEST-WORKING MUSCLES IN THE BODY, CONTRACTING AT LEAST 20,000 TIMES A DAY!

THE DIAPHRAGM IS NOT THE ONLY MUSCLE INVOLVED IN BREATHING. IT GETS HELP FROM THE INTERCOSTAL MUSCLES, WHICH ARE LOCATED BETWEEN THE RIBS. THEY HELP PULL THE RIBCAGE UPWARDS!

WHEN WE INHALE THE DIAPHRAGM CONTRACTS (SQUEEZES FLATTER) AND MOVES DOWNWARDS. AT THE SAME TIME, THE INTERCOSTAL MUSCLES LIFT THE RIBCAGE UP AND OUTWARDS. THIS GIVES THE LUNGS MORE ROOM TO INFLATE (BECOME LARGER) AND PULL AIR FROM OUTSIDE THE BODY INTO IT.

WHEN WE EXHALE THE DIAPHRAGM RELAXES AND MOVES BACK UP AND THE INTERCOSTAL MUSCLES RELAX PULLING THE RIBCAGE DOWN AND INWARDS. THE LUNGS RETURN TO THEIR DEFLATED, SMALLER SIZE, WHICH PUSHES THE AIR OUT OF THEM.

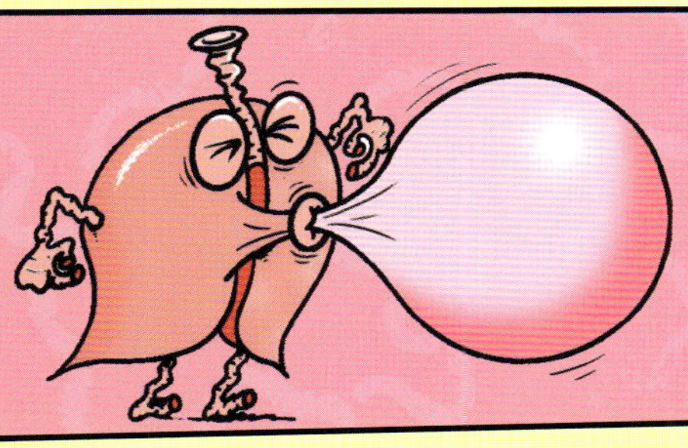

A lot more energy is needed to breathe in than to breathe out. Think about how hard it is to blow up a balloon but how easily the balloon deflates when you let the air out.

GAS EXCHANGE AND THE LUNGS

Every cell in our body needs oxygen to generate energy to live, and we get this from the air we breathe. The main job of the respiratory system is to bring fresh air with plenty of oxygen into the body and to remove carbon dioxide, the waste by-product of respiration.

DID YOU KNOW?

The average person breathes in the equivalent of just over seven litres of air every minute and takes around 17,000 breaths per day!

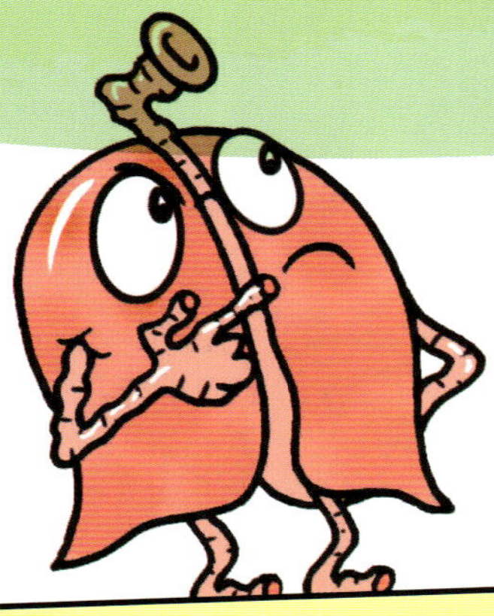

When the air breathed in reaches the alveoli in the lungs, an exchange of gases takes place by a process called diffusion.

Diffusion is the movement of a substance, like a gas, from an area of high concentration to an area of low concentration.

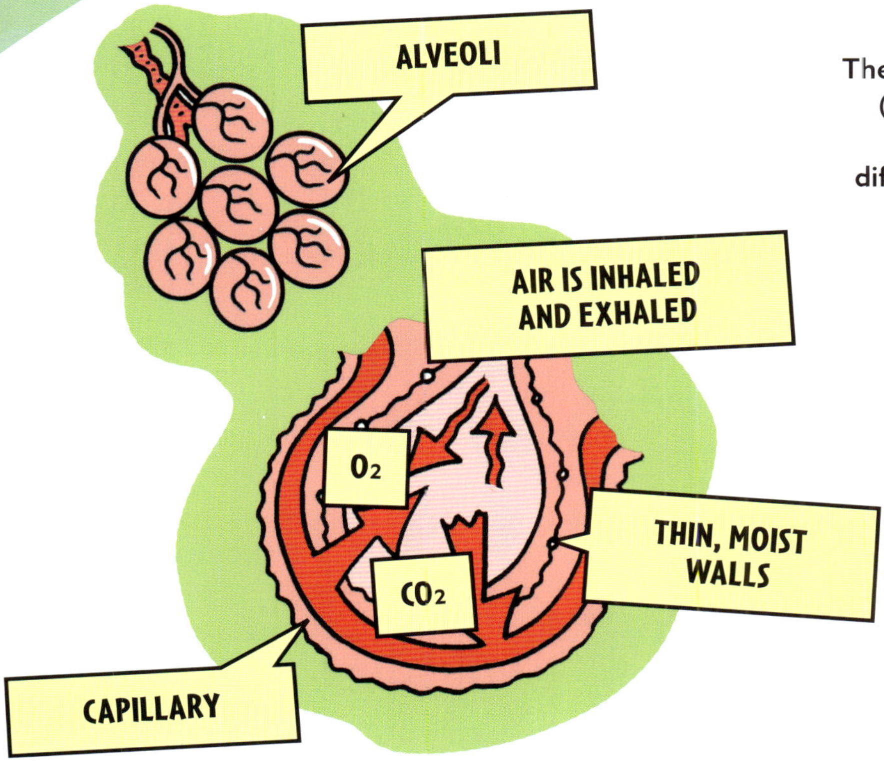

The walls of the alveoli are incredibly thin (about one hundredth of the thickness of a human hair!) and moist to allow diffusion to take place easily. They contain tiny blood vessels called capillaries.

DID YOU KNOW?

The air we exhale contains tiny particles of water, and every day we exhale almost half a litre of water!

THE OXYGEN IN THE ALVEOLI MOVES INTO THE BLOOD IN THE CAPILLARIES, WHERE IT ATTACHES ITSELF TO A SUBSTANCE CALLED HAEMOGLOBIN IN THE RED BLOOD CELLS.
AS THE BLOOD TRAVELS AROUND THE BODY, THESE CELLS DELIVER THE OXYGEN TO ALL THE ORGANS THAT NEED IT.

CARBON DIOXIDE, A WASTE GAS, IS PRODUCED AS A PART OF THIS PROCESS. IT IS RETURNED TO THE LUNGS IN THE BLOOD, WHERE IT PASSES THROUGH THE WALLS OF THE CAPILLARIES INTO THE ALVEOLI. HERE IT IS REMOVED AND EXHALED WHEN WE BREATHE OUT.

The blood then takes up the oxygen from the air in the alveoli that has been breathed in (inhaled) and the process starts over again.

BLOOD CIRCULATION AND THE LUNGS

1. Blood travels around the body in tubes called blood vessels. These blood vessels include arteries, veins and capillaries. This is our circulatory system.

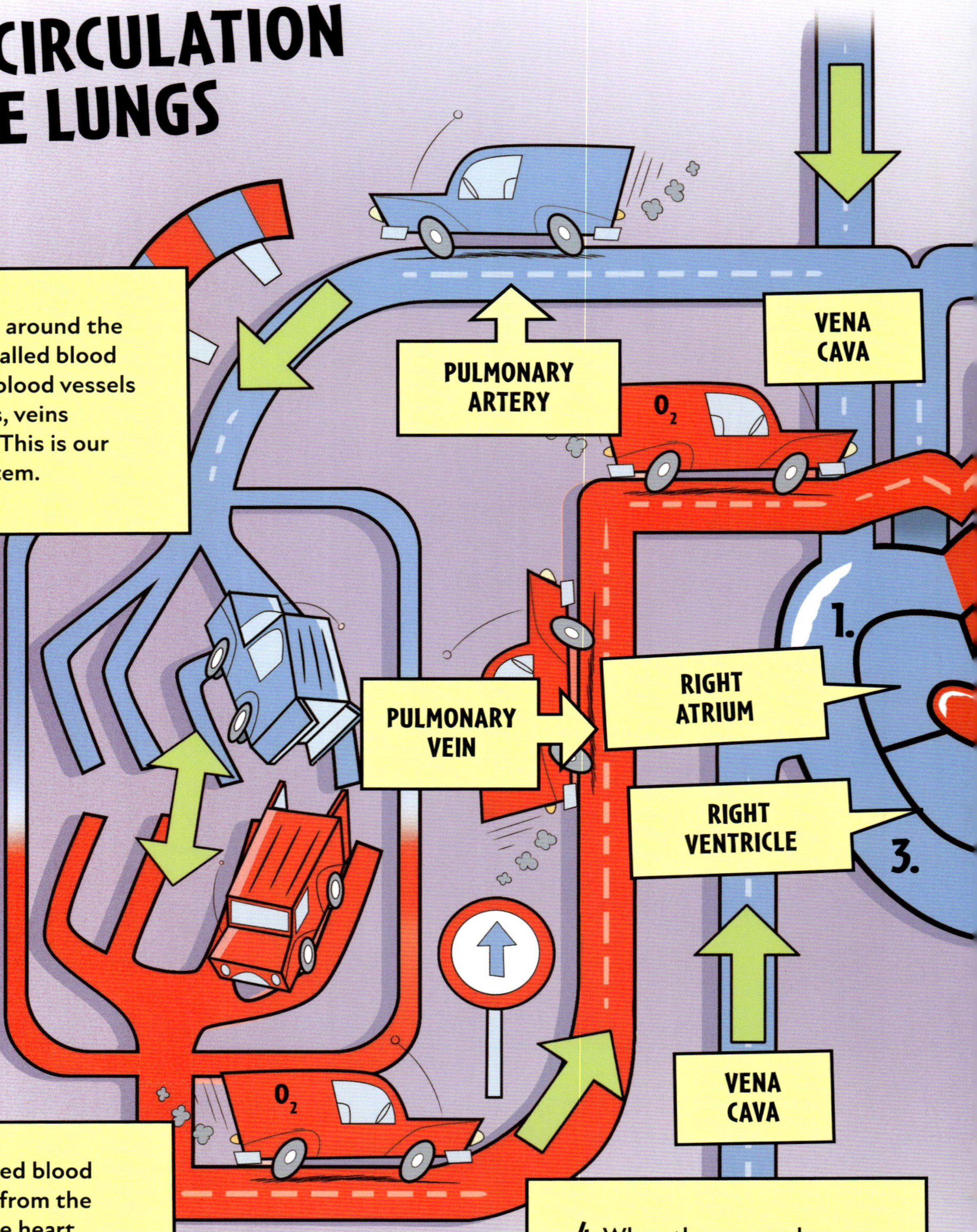

2. Deoxygenated blood is transported from the right side of the heart into the lungs, where it picks up oxygen.

4. When the oxygen has been delivered to all the organs, the deoxygenated blood travels back to the right side of the heart and the cycle begins again.

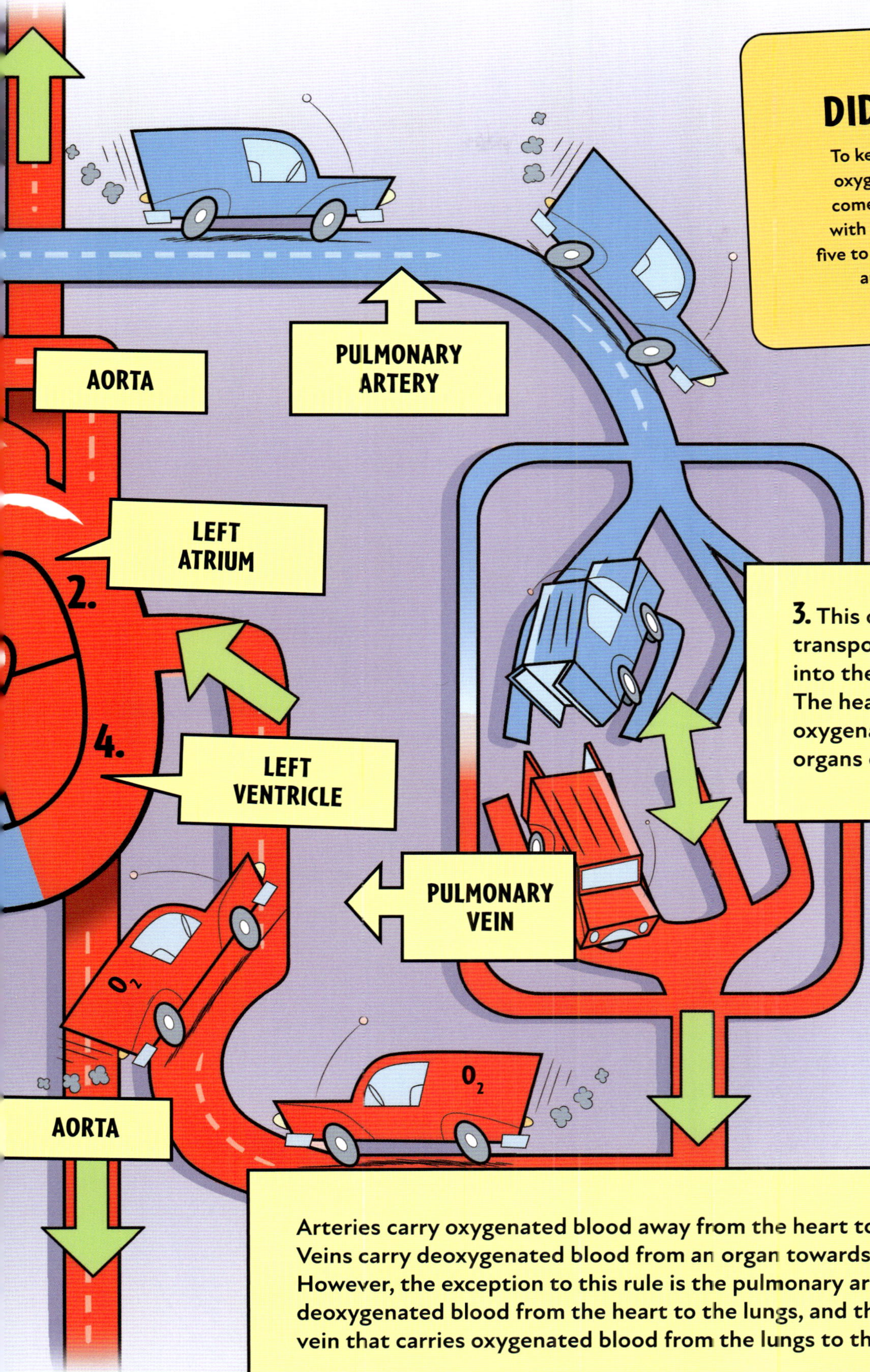

DID YOU KNOW?

To keep the body supplied with oxygen, a lot of blood needs to come into proximity (closeness) with the alveoli. This means that five to six litres of blood go through an adult's lungs a minute!

3. This oxygenated blood is transported from the lungs into the left side of the heart. The heart then pumps the oxygenated blood to all the organs of the body.

Arteries carry oxygenated blood away from the heart towards an organ. Veins carry deoxygenated blood from an organ towards the heart. However, the exception to this rule is the pulmonary artery that carries deoxygenated blood from the heart to the lungs, and the pulmonary vein that carries oxygenated blood from the lungs to the heart.

LUNG INFECTIONS

The respiratory system is like a finely tuned machine with all the various parts working together to help us breathe. But, like all machines, sometimes things break down. The most common cause of this is infection.

We breathe in between 100,000 and 1 million microbes a day including bacteria, viruses and fungi!

Fortunately, the lungs have several ways to keep the mob of microbes out and to deal with any invaders that may breach the defences. They have outside help too.

WHAT ARE MICROBES?

Microbes (also called micro-organisms) are tiny living things that are found all around us. They live in the air, in water and in soil and in our bodies too. They are too small to be seen by the naked eye but can be seen under a microscope.

Some microbes are beneficial, such as those that produce antibiotics or are used in food preparation; others are harmful and can cause diseases.

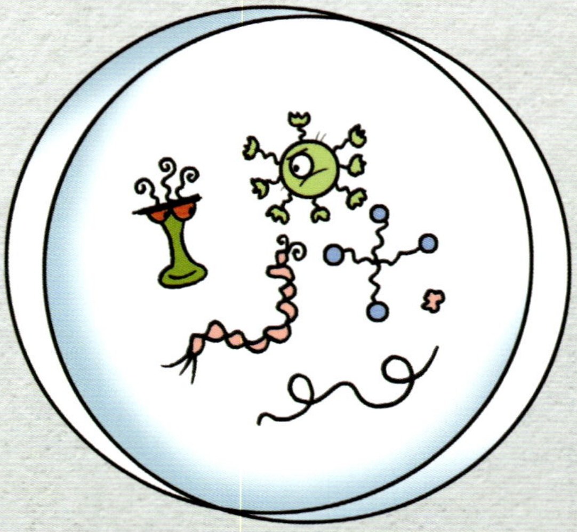

DEFENCES

Mucus throughout the airways traps some of these micro-organisms. There are enzymes within the mucus that can destroy the invading microbes. The cilia beat more than 1,000 times a minute to sweep the mucus up the airway towards the throat, to be swallowed or coughed up if necessary.

If infectious microbes do manage to get past the mucus, then a second line of defence is activated. Special white blood cells surround the microbes and destroy them before they can do any harm.

COUGHS VS SNEEZES

A SNEEZE HAPPENS WHEN THERE IS IRRITATION OF THE NASAL HAIRS BY PARTICLES OR INFECTIONS SUCH AS VIRUSES. A SNEEZE CAN PROPEL AIR PARTICLES AT SPEEDS OF UP TO 160 KMPH!

COUGHING HAPPENS WHEN SOMETHING IRRITATES THE AIRWAYS. IT HELPS PREVENT MICROBES FROM ATTACHING TO THE INSIDE OF THE LUNGS. A COUGH CAN PROPEL PARTICLES AND AIR OUT OF THE LUNGS AT SPEEDS OF UP TO 80 KMPH!

REMEMBER

Always cover your mouth and nose when you cough and sneeze, and then wash your hands, to stop the harmful germs in the mucus spreading onto other surfaces.

WHEN THE DEFENCES FAIL

When the respiratory system's defences fail, we can develop infections anywhere in the respiratory tract including the airways and the lungs.

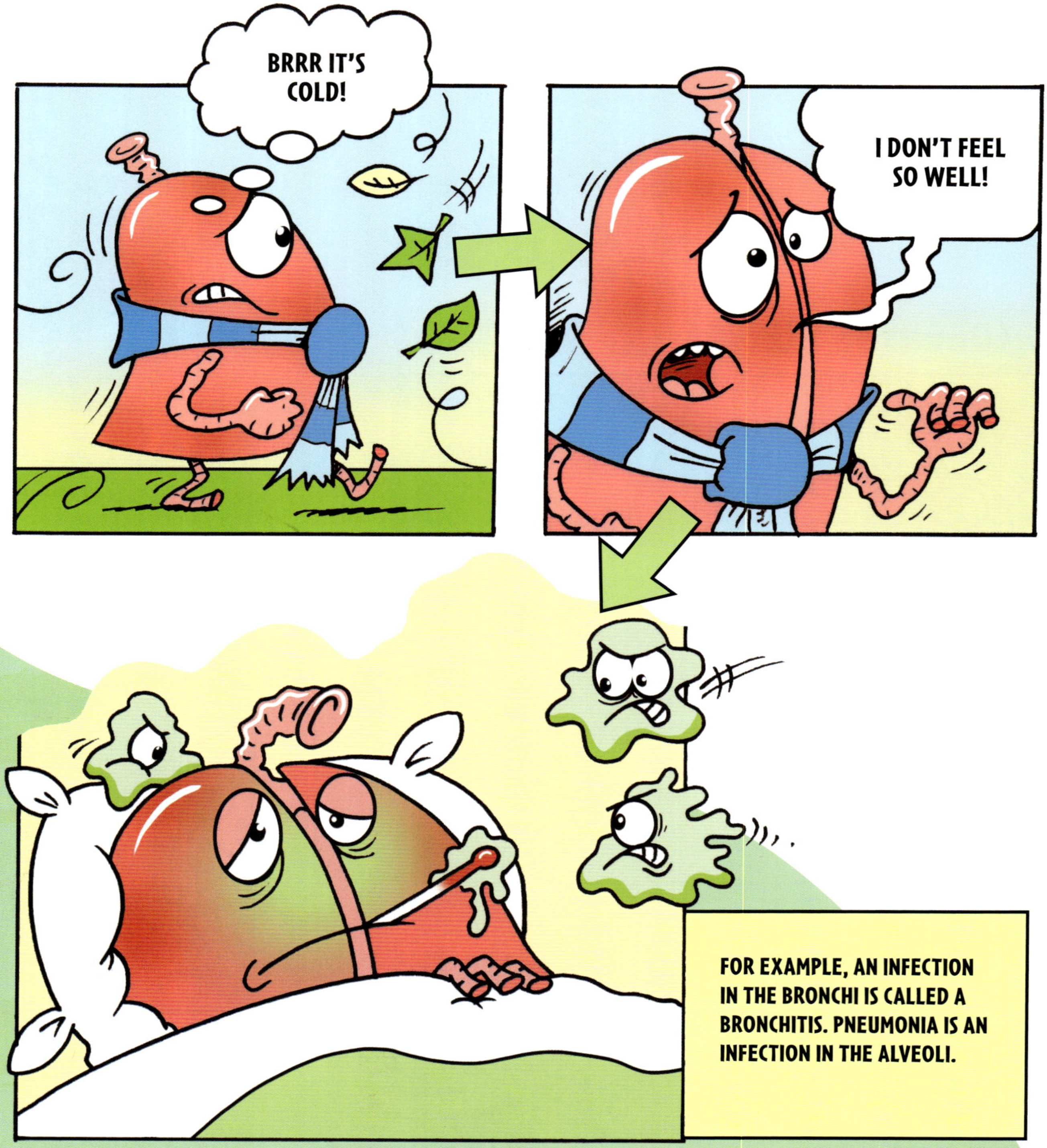

DID YOU KNOW?

When the lungs become infected the sputum can become green, rather than its usual clear colour. This happens because white blood cells release a special enzyme that helps destroy bacteria. This enzyme gives the sputum a green colour.

WHY DO THE DEFENCES FAIL?

THIS SOMETIMES OCCURS WHEN VAST NUMBERS OF EXTERNAL MICROBES OVERWHELM THE DEFENCE MECHANISMS ...

... OR BY CHANCE WHEN SOMETHING UNEXPECTED HAPPENS HAPPENS.

ASTHMA ATTACK

One of the most common lung illnesses is asthma. People with asthma get attacks when their airways suddenly become very tight. This usually happens when the person breathes in certain particles like dust, pollen, pet hair or smoke.

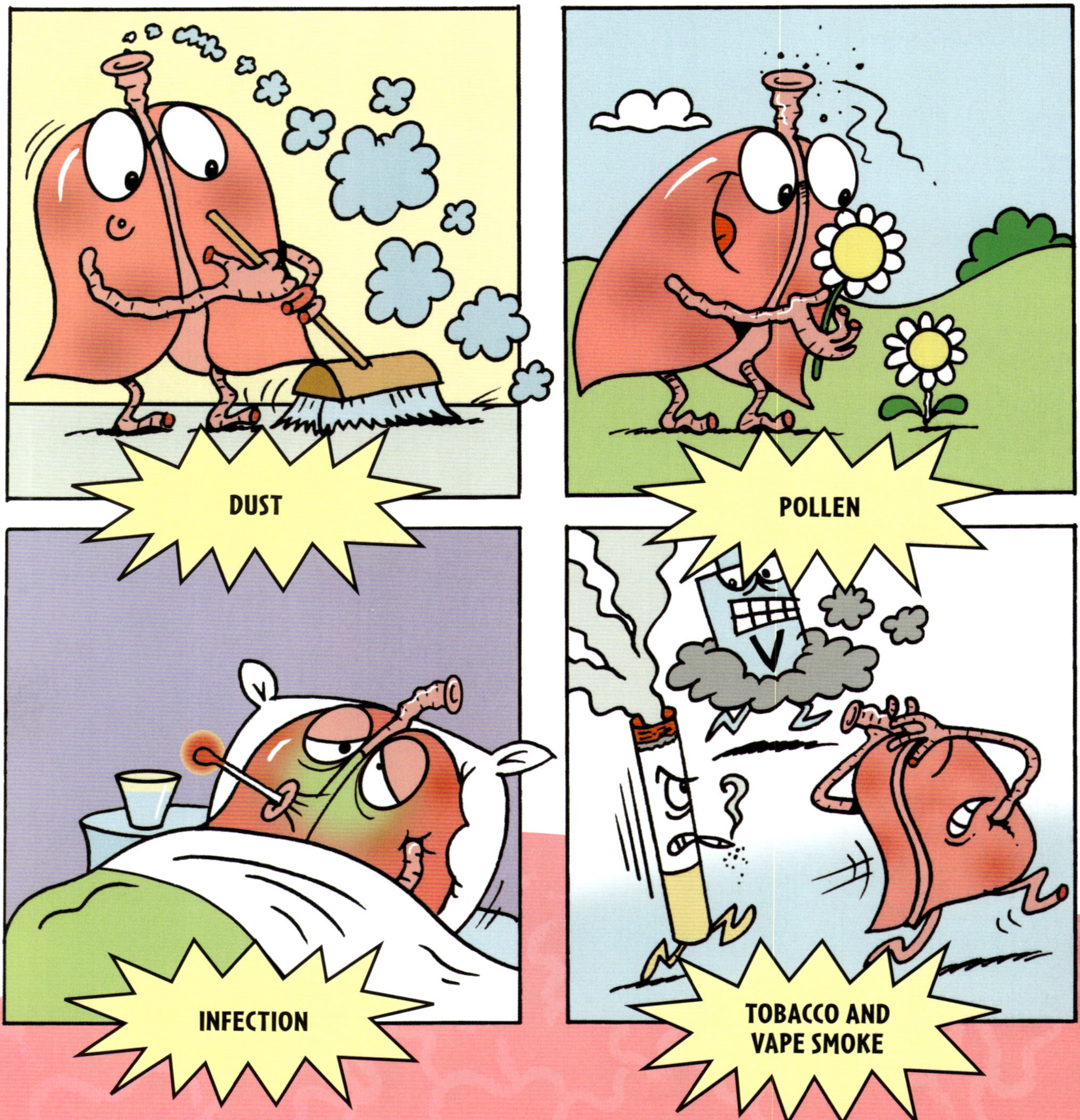

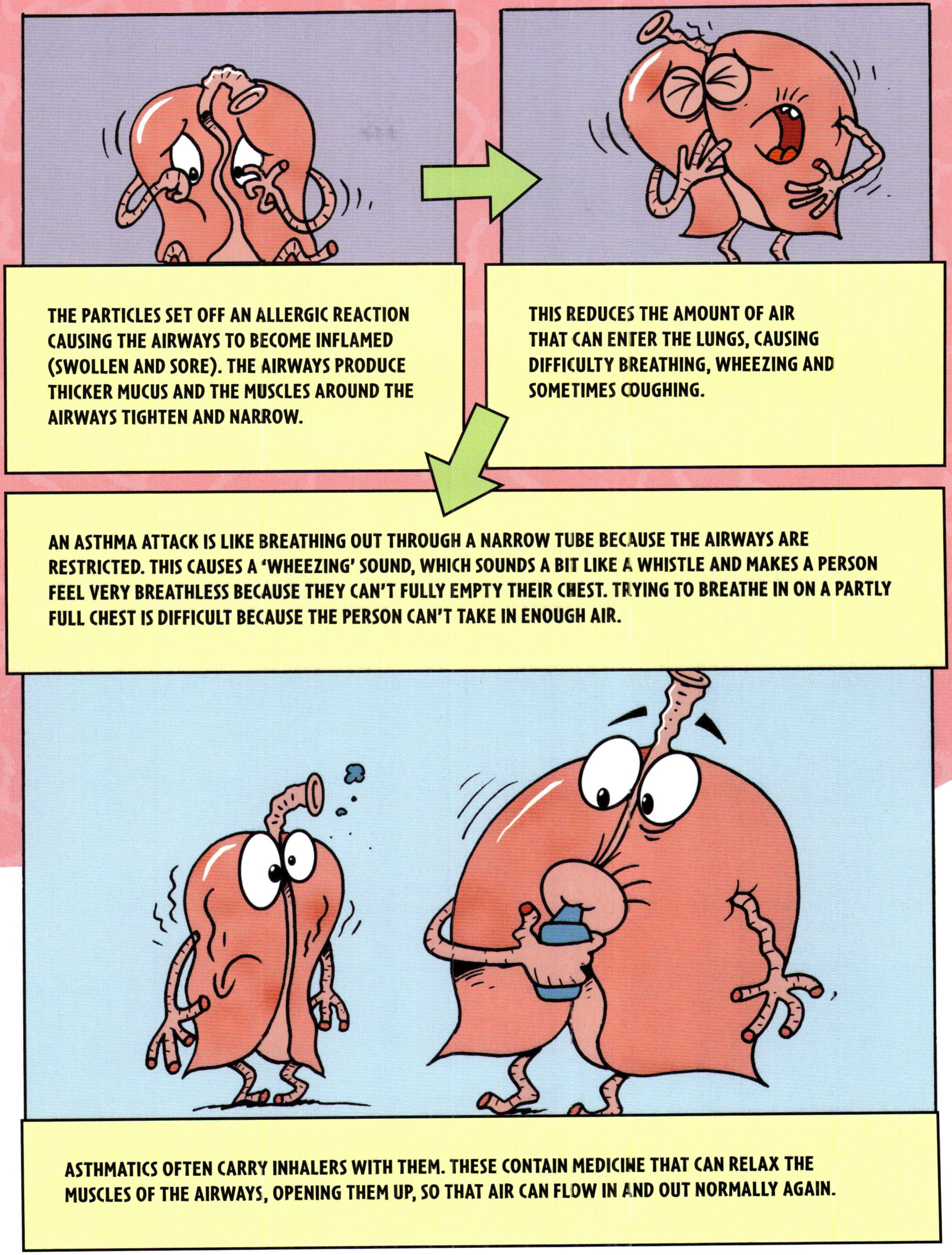
THE PARTICLES SET OFF AN ALLERGIC REACTION CAUSING THE AIRWAYS TO BECOME INFLAMED (SWOLLEN AND SORE). THE AIRWAYS PRODUCE THICKER MUCUS AND THE MUSCLES AROUND THE AIRWAYS TIGHTEN AND NARROW.
THIS REDUCES THE AMOUNT OF AIR THAT CAN ENTER THE LUNGS, CAUSING DIFFICULTY BREATHING, WHEEZING AND SOMETIMES COUGHING.
AN ASTHMA ATTACK IS LIKE BREATHING OUT THROUGH A NARROW TUBE BECAUSE THE AIRWAYS ARE RESTRICTED. THIS CAUSES A 'WHEEZING' SOUND, WHICH SOUNDS A BIT LIKE A WHISTLE AND MAKES A PERSON FEEL VERY BREATHLESS BECAUSE THEY CAN'T FULLY EMPTY THEIR CHEST. TRYING TO BREATHE IN ON A PARTLY FULL CHEST IS DIFFICULT BECAUSE THE PERSON CAN'T TAKE IN ENOUGH AIR.
ASTHMATICS OFTEN CARRY INHALERS WITH THEM. THESE CONTAIN MEDICINE THAT CAN RELAX THE MUSCLES OF THE AIRWAYS, OPENING THEM UP, SO THAT AIR CAN FLOW IN AND OUT NORMALLY AGAIN.

BREATHE IN ... BREATHE OUT ...

Sometimes when we feel anxious, emotional or a bit upset our breathing can become affected. Instead of our usual steady, calm breaths in and out that we make without thinking, our breathing can become quicker and more laboured, and we are more conscious of it.

There are several breathing techniques that can be practised and used to return your breathing to normal and to calm your anxieties. Why not try them out!

TRIANGLE BREATHING

As the name suggests, triangle breathing involves breathing keeping the number three (the number of sides of a triangle) in mind. You can sit or stand to do this exercise.

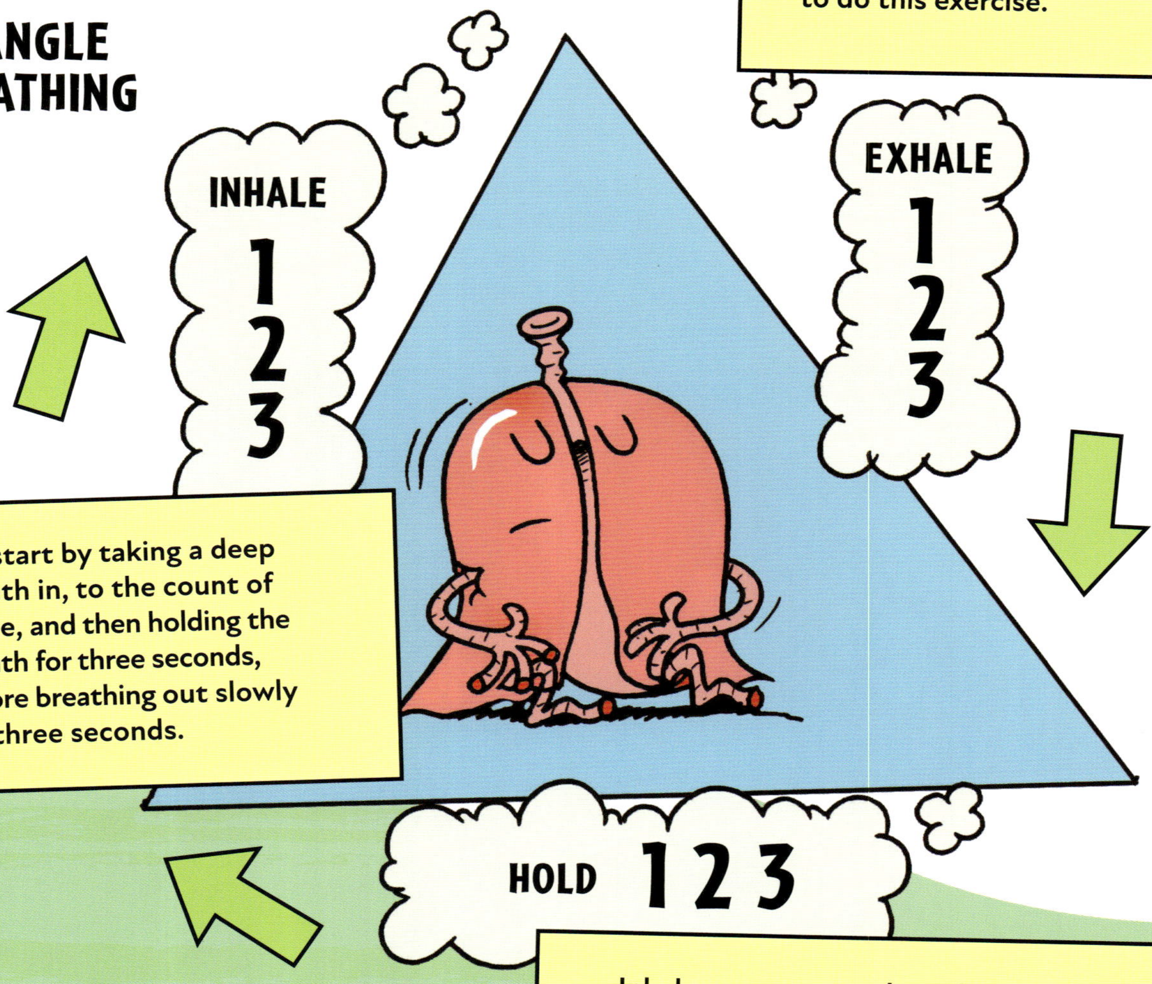

So, start by taking a deep breath in, to the count of three, and then holding the breath for three seconds, before breathing out slowly for three seconds.

Inhale one ... two ... three, hold one ... two ... three, exhale one ... two ... three. Repeat the triangle sequence four or five times until you feel calm.

CANDLE BREATHING

This technique involves visualising blowing out candles on a birthday cake. Imagine that you have a birthday cake in front of you covered in candles. Take a deep breath in through your nose and then exhale out through your mouth as if you are blowing out the candles on the cake.

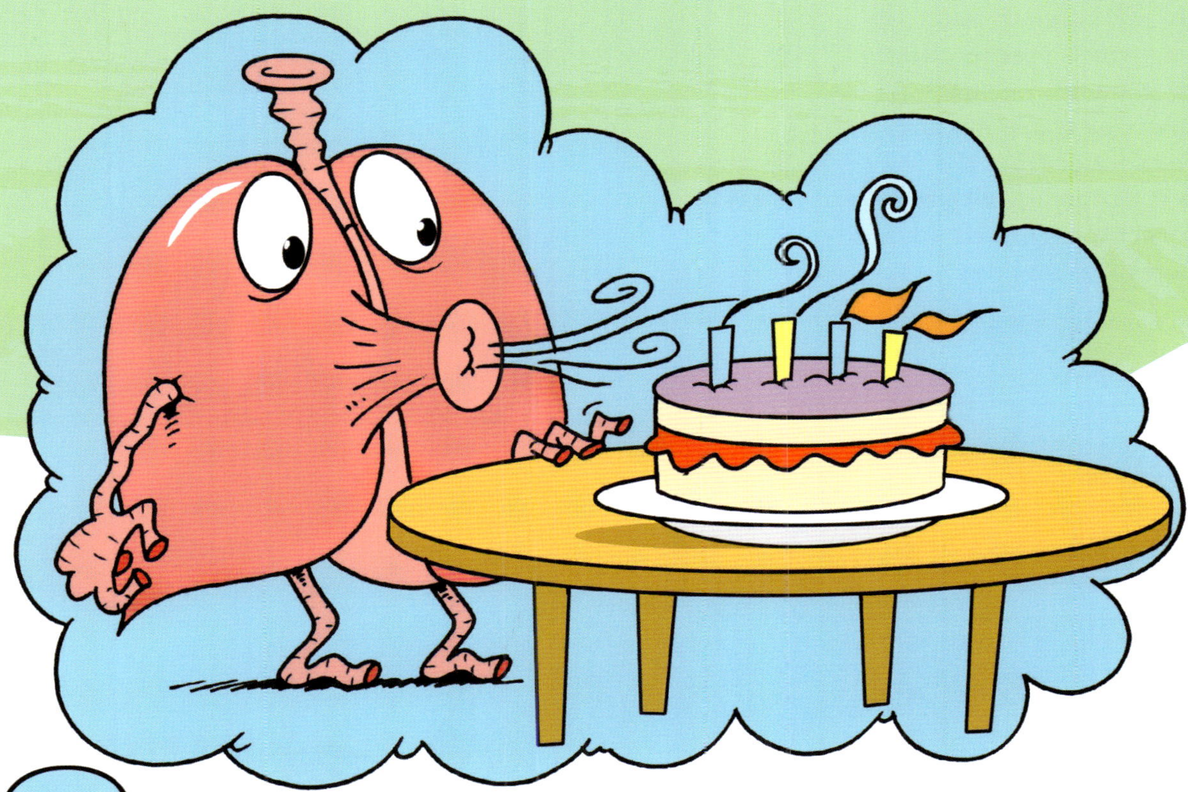

Repeat four or five times until you feel calm. You can even make a wish while you are doing the breathing!

EXAMINING THE LUNGS

We have several tools for examining the lungs and detecting if things are going wrong.

A doctor will listen to your breathing with a stethoscope to see if it sounds normal. A stethoscope transmits and amplifies sounds from the chest. If there is a problem with the lungs, a doctor might hear sounds of wheezes and crackles.

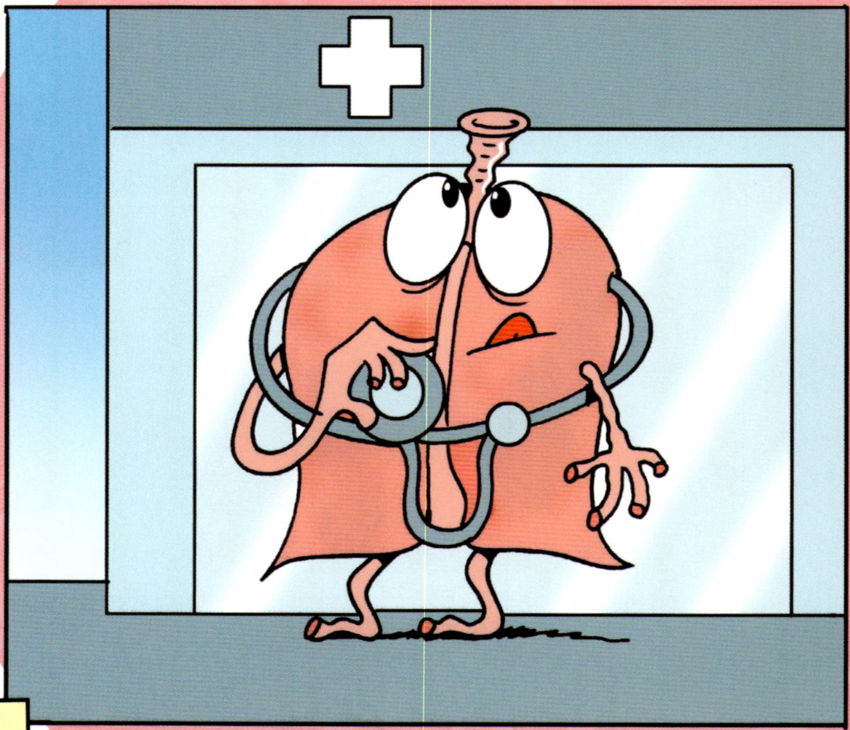

Sometimes a doctor will place a small device called a pulse oximeter on your fingertip or ear.

This device measures the levels of oxygen carried on the haemoglobin in the blood.

WITH SOME RESPIRATORY PROBLEMS, IT MAY WELL BE NECESSARY TO TAKE A PICTURE OF THE LUNGS. THIS CAN BE DONE WITH EITHER A CHEST X-RAY WHICH TAKES A TWO-DIMENSIONAL IMAGE OF THE LUNGS.

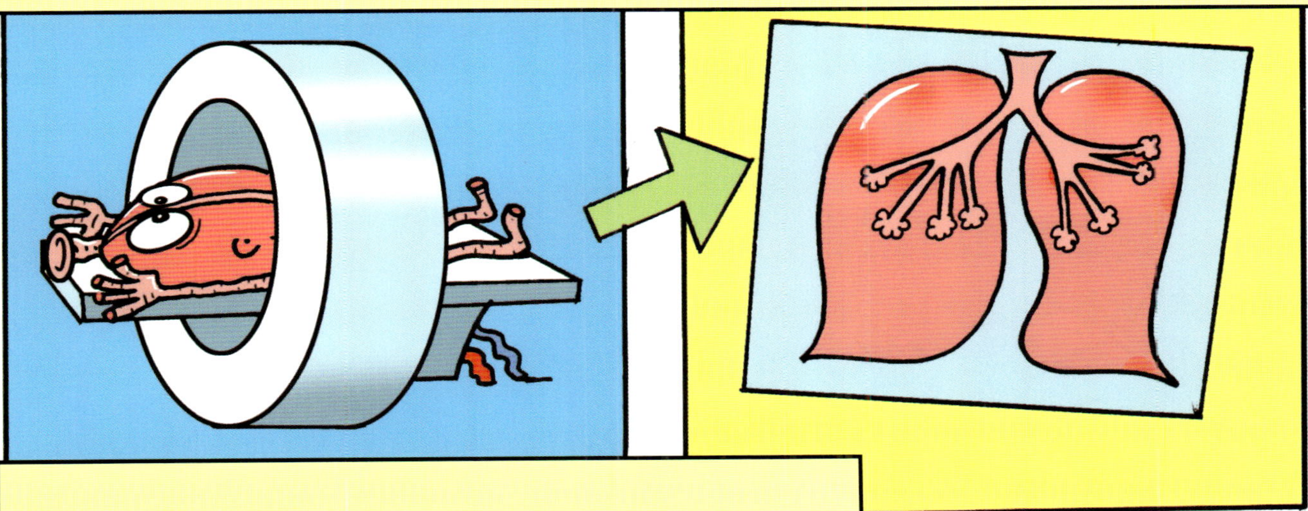

OR A THREE-DIMENSIONAL PICTURE CAN BE TAKEN USING A CT SCAN.

DID YOU KNOW?

The first stethoscope on record was invented in 1816 and it was no more than rolled up paper in the form of a funnel! You can try making your own and listening to someone's heartbeat and lungs.

HEALTHY LUNGS

THERE ARE LOTS OF THINGS YOU CAN DO TO KEEP YOUR LUNGS HEALTHY.

• DON'T SMOKE OR VAPE. INHALING CIGARETTE SMOKE EVEN FROM OTHER PEOPLE IS VERY HARMFUL FOR YOUR LUNGS. THE CHEMICALS DAMAGE THE LUNG TISSUES AND MAKE IT HARDER TO BREATHE.

• EXERCISE AND KEEP ACTIVE. WHEN YOU EXERCISE YOUR LUNGS AND HEART WORK HARD TO BRING OXYGEN INTO YOUR BODY AND TO DELIVER IT TO THE MUSCLES YOU ARE USING. THIS IMPROVES YOUR BLOOD CIRCULATION AND STRENGTHENS THE MUSCLES AROUND THE LUNGS, ALLOWING YOU TO BREATHE MORE EASILY WHEN YOU ARE ACTIVE.

• EAT HEALTHY FOOD. THE VITAMINS AND MINERALS IN HEALTHY FOOD WILL BOOST YOUR IMMUNE SYSTEM AND HELP KEEP YOUR RESPIRATORY SYSTEM WORKING EFFICIENTLY.

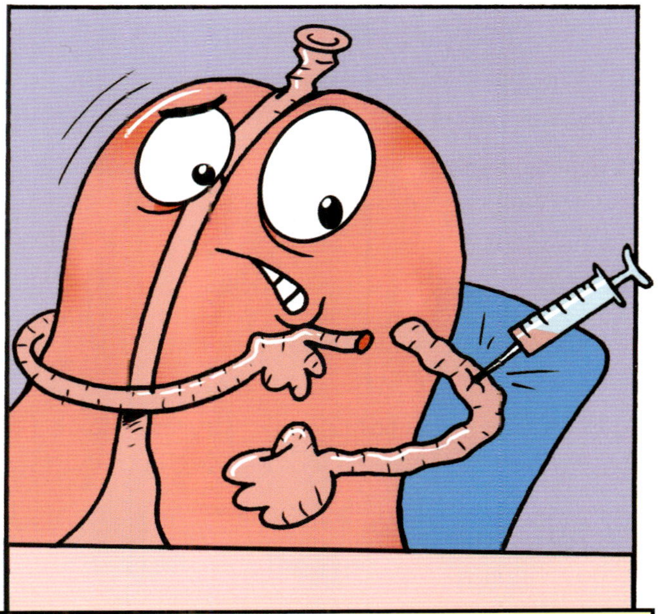

• YOUR GROWN-UPS NEED TO MAKE SURE YOU HAVE ALL THE VACCINATIONS YOUR DOCTOR SAYS YOU NEED.

• VACCINES PREVENT INFECTIONS BY TRICKING THE BODY THAT IT IS FACING AN INFECTION. VACCINES INTRODUCE A SMALL PART OF THE GERM OR A DEAD GERM. THIS WAY WHEN THE BODY HAS TO FIGHT THE REAL INFECTION, IT IS READY AND ALWAYS HAS THE WEAPONS IT NEEDS TO PROTECT ITSELF.

GLOSSARY

atria (atrium,singular) – the left and right upper chambers of the heart.

bronchi (bronchus, singular) – the branches of the trachea that lead into the lungs. 'Broncho' comes from the Greek word 'brónchos', meaning 'windpipe', another name for the trachea.

deoxygenated blood – blood that is low on oxygen.

enzyme – a substance that speeds up a chemical reaction in living organisms without being changed by the reaction.

haemoglobin – a special protein in the red blood cells that contains iron, and which carries oxygen from the lungs to all parts of the body.

neurons (neuron, singular) – cells that receive and send messages from the body to the brain and back to the body. They are also called nerve cells. A bundle of neurons is called a nerve.

oxygenated blood – blood that is rich in oxygen.

red blood cells – the red component of the blood which brings oxygen to all parts of the body and takes carbon dioxide back to the lungs where it is exhaled. In an adult human there are over five million red cells in one cubic millimetre of blood.

ventricles (ventricle, singular) – the left and right lower chambers of the heart.

white blood cells – the cells in the blood that help defend our body from infections.

INDEX